HAL•LEONARD
INSTRUMENTAL PLAY-ALONG

TENOR SAX

AUDIO ACCESS INCLUDED

PLAYBACK+
Speed • Pitch • Balance • Loop

JAZZ CLASSICS

T0039682

Audio arrangements by Peter Deneff

To access audio visit:
www.halleonard.com/mylibrary
Enter Code
7096-8627-2381-9936

ISBN 978-1-4950-4750-3

HAL•LEONARD®
7777 W. BLUEMOUND RD. P.O. BOX 13819 MILWAUKEE, WI 53213

For all works contained herein:
Unauthorized copying, arranging, adapting, recording, Internet posting, public performance,
or other distribution of the printed or recorded music in this publication is an infringement of copyright.
Infringers are liable under the law.

Visit Hal Leonard Online at
www.halleonard.com

DOXY

TENOR SAX

By SONNY ROLLINS

Copyright © 1963 Prestige Music c/o The Bicycle Music Company
Copyright Renewed
International Copyright Secured   All Rights Reserved

IN WALKED BUD

TENOR SAX

By THELONIOUS MONK

Copyright © 1948 (Renewed) by Embassy Music Corporation (BMI)
International Copyright Secured   All Rights Reserved
Reprinted by Permission

IN YOUR OWN SWEET WAY

TENOR SAX

By DAVE BRUBECK

Copyright © 1955, 1956 by Derry Music Co.
Copyright Renewed
Sole Selling Agent: Shawnee Press, Inc.
International Copyright Secured   All Rights Reserved
Reprinted by Permission

MERCY, MERCY, MERCY

TENOR SAX

Composed by JOSEF ZAWINUL

Easy Soul beat

Copyright © 1966 Zawinul Enterprises LLC
Copyright Renewed
All Rights Administered by Songs Of Kobalt Music Publishing
All Rights Reserved   Used by Permission

NARDIS

TENOR SAX

By MILES DAVIS

Copyright © 1959 Jazz Horn Music Corporation
Copyright Renewed
All Rights Administered by Songs Of Kobalt Music Publishing
All Rights Reserved   Used by Permission

ON GREEN DOLPHIN STREET

TENOR SAX

Lyrics by NED WASHINGTON
Music by BRONISLAU KAPER

© 1947 (Renewed) Catharine Hinen Music, Patti Washington Music and Primary Wave Songs
All Rights for Catharine Hinen Music Controlled by Shapiro, Bernstein & Co., Inc.
All Rights for Primary Wave Songs Controlled by EMI April Music Inc. (Publishing) and Alfred Music (Print)
All Rights Reserved   Used by Permission

REUNION BLUES

TENOR SAX

By MILT JACKSON

Copyright © 1962 (Renewed 1990) by MJQ Music, Inc.
All Rights Administered by Hal Leonard - Milwin Music Corp.
International Copyright Secured   All Rights Reserved

STOLEN MOMENTS

TENOR SAX

Words and Music by
OLIVER NELSON

Copyright © 1962, 1965 by Noslen Music Co. LLC
Copyright Renewed
All Rights for the World Administered by Alameda Music Company
International Copyright Secured   All Rights Reserved
Used by Permission

ST. THOMAS

TENOR SAX

By SONNY ROLLINS

Copyright © 1963 Prestige Music c/o The Bicycle Music Company
Copyright Renewed
International Copyright Secured   All Rights Reserved

SCRAPPLE FROM THE APPLE

TENOR SAX

By CHARLIE PARKER

Copyright © 1957 (Renewed 1985) Atlantic Music Corp.
International Copyright Secured   All Rights Reserved

SIDEWINDER

TENOR SAX

By LEE MORGAN

Copyright © 1959 (Renewed) Conrad Music (BMI)
U.S. Rights owned by Arc/Conrad Music LLC (Administered by BMG Rights Management (US) LLC)
International Copyright Secured   All Rights Reserved

TAKE FIVE

TENOR SAX

By PAUL DESMOND

© 1960 (Renewed 1988) Desmond Music Company
All Rights outside the USA Controlled by Derry Music Company
International Copyright Secured   All Rights Reserved

23

HAL·LEONARD INSTRUMENTAL PLAY-ALONG

Your favorite songs are arranged just for solo instrumentalists with this outstanding series. Each book includes a great full-accompaniment play-along audio so you can sound just like a pro! Check out **www.halleonard.com** to see all the titles available.

The Beatles

All You Need Is Love • Blackbird • Day Tripper • Eleanor Rigby • Get Back • Here, There and Everywhere • Hey Jude • I Will • Let It Be • Lucy in the Sky with Diamonds • Ob-La-Di, Ob-La-Da • Penny Lane • Something • Ticket to Ride • Yesterday.

____	00225330	Flute	$14.99
____	00225331	Clarinet	$14.99
____	00225332	Alto Sax	$14.99
____	00225333	Tenor Sax	$14.99
____	00225334	Trumpet	$14.99
____	00225335	Horn	$14.99
____	00225336	Trombone	$14.99
____	00225337	Violin	$14.99
____	00225338	Viola	$14.99
____	00225339	Cello	$14.99

Chart Hits

All About That Bass • All of Me • Happy • Radioactive • Roar • Say Something • Shake It Off • A Sky Full of Stars • Someone like You • Stay with Me • Thinking Out Loud • Uptown Funk.

____	00146207	Flute	$12.99
____	00146208	Clarinet	$12.99
____	00146209	Alto Sax	$12.99
____	00146210	Tenor Sax	$12.99
____	00146211	Trumpet	$12.99
____	00146212	Horn	$12.99
____	00146213	Trombone	$12.99
____	00146214	Violin	$12.99
____	00146215	Viola	$12.99
____	00146216	Cello	$12.99

Coldplay

Clocks • Every Teardrop Is a Waterfall • Fix You • In My Place • Lost! • Paradise • The Scientist • Speed of Sound • Trouble • Violet Hill • Viva La Vida • Yellow.

____	00103337	Flute	$12.99
____	00103338	Clarinet	$12.99
____	00103339	Alto Sax	$12.99
____	00103340	Tenor Sax	$12.99
____	00103341	Trumpet	$12.99
____	00103342	Horn	$12.99
____	00103343	Trombone	$12.99
____	00103344	Violin	$12.99
____	00103345	Viola	$12.99
____	00103346	Cello	$12.99

Disney Greats

Arabian Nights • Hawaiian Roller Coaster Ride • It's a Small World • Look Through My Eyes • Yo Ho (A Pirate's Life for Me) • and more.

____	00841934	Flute	$12.99
____	00841935	Clarinet	$12.99
____	00841936	Alto Sax	$12.99
____	00841937	Tenor Sax	$12.95
____	00841938	Trumpet	$12.99
____	00841939	Horn	$12.99
____	00841940	Trombone	$12.95
____	00841941	Violin	$12.99
____	00841942	Viola	$12.99
____	00841943	Cello	$12.99
____	00842078	Oboe	$12.99

Great Themes

Bella's Lullaby • Chariots of Fire • Get Smart • Hawaii Five-O Theme • I Love Lucy • The Odd Couple • Spanish Flea • and more.

____	00842468	Flute	$12.99
____	00842469	Clarinet	$12.99
____	00842470	Alto Sax	$12.99
____	00842471	Tenor Sax	$12.99
____	00842472	Trumpet	$12.99
____	00842473	Horn	$12.99
____	00842474	Trombone	$12.99
____	00842475	Violin	$12.99
____	00842476	Viola	$12.99
____	00842477	Cello	$12.99

Popular Hits

Breakeven • Fireflies • Halo • Hey, Soul Sister • I Gotta Feeling • I'm Yours • Need You Now • Poker Face • Viva La Vida • You Belong with Me • and more.

____	00842511	Flute	$12.99
____	00842512	Clarinet	$12.99
____	00842513	Alto Sax	$12.99
____	00842514	Tenor Sax	$12.99
____	00842515	Trumpet	$12.99
____	00842516	Horn	$12.99
____	00842517	Trombone	$12.99
____	00842518	Violin	$12.99
____	00842519	Viola	$12.99
____	00842520	Cello	$12.99

Songs from Frozen, Tangled and Enchanted

Do You Want to Build a Snowman? • For the First Time in Forever • Happy Working Song • I See the Light • In Summer • Let It Go • Mother Knows Best • That's How You Know • True Love's First Kiss • When Will My Life Begin • and more.

____	00126921	Flute	$14.99
____	00126922	Clarinet	$14.99
____	00126923	Alto Sax	$14.99
____	00126924	Tenor Sax	$14.99
____	00126925	Trumpet	$14.99
____	00126926	Horn	$14.99
____	00126927	Trombone	$14.99
____	00126928	Violin	$14.99
____	00126929	Viola	$14.99
____	00126930	Cello	$14.99

Top Hits

Adventure of a Lifetime • Budapest • Die a Happy Man • Ex's & Oh's • Fight Song • Hello • Let It Go • Love Yourself • One Call Away • Pillowtalk • Stitches • Writing's on the Wall.

____	00171073	Flute	$12.99
____	00171074	Clarinet	$12.99
____	00171075	Alto Sax	$12.99
____	00171106	Tenor Sax	$12.99
____	00171107	Trumpet	$12.99
____	00171108	Horn	$12.99
____	00171109	Trombone	$12.99
____	00171110	Violin	$12.99
____	00171111	Viola	$12.99
____	00171112	Cello	$12.99

Wicked

As Long As You're Mine • Dancing Through Life • Defying Gravity • For Good • I'm Not That Girl • Popular • The Wizard and I • and more.

____	00842236	Flute	$12.99
____	00842237	Clarinet	$12.99
____	00842238	Alto Saxophone	$11.95
____	00842239	Tenor Saxophone	$11.95
____	00842240	Trumpet	$11.99
____	00842241	Horn	$11.95
____	00842242	Trombone	$12.99
____	00842243	Violin	$11.99
____	00842244	Viola	$12.99
____	00842245	Cello	$12.99

Prices, contents, and availability subject to change without notice.
Disney characters and artwork © Disney Enterprises, Inc.

HAL·LEONARD®

0617